WITNESS

WITNESS

By Beau Beausoleil

Cover & Drawings
by Sheila King

Panjandrum Press, Inc.
San Francisco 1976

Some of these poems have appeared in the following magazines:
*Abraxas, Chicago Review, Gallimaufry, Invisible City,
Isthmus, Marilyn, Panjandrum* and *Poetry Flash.*

First Printing: September, 1976
Second Printing: 1978
Manufactured in the United States of America

Library of Congress Cataloging in Publication Data

Beausoleil, Beau, 1941-
 Witness.

 I. Title.
PS3552.E232W5   811'.5'4   76-39971
ISBN 0-915572-23-0

*This book was made possible in part by
a grant from the National Endowment for the Arts, a Federal Agency.*

Panjandrum Press, Inc.
99 Sanchez Street
San Francisco, California 94114

First Printing: September, 1976
Manufactured in the United States of America

Note

The spine of Beausoleil's poems is drawn
from all the wars of guitars since Lorca's
flamencan one, made to lean against the
thumb of the reader's imagination in
that half-lit stoney *cave* where – these
days – we all perform. Beausoleil quests
for that center of the cube (of met-
aphoric ism? of acid?) where ice is hot
and the temperature of the eyes and
ears can be valid notations. No other
San Francisco poet moves with such
controlled grace through the fretted repetitions of french/spanish "surrealism"
to praise what such repetitions really
are: field rows, landscape, country that
city men discover their need for in the
sophisticated plough of the poem.

–*Jack Hirschman*

Witness

The different horses
of our sex
overtake us

We hammer
at the night

We chew a leaf
of stars
we spit
until
the pressure of sight
is removed

Until
the floor
sheds our feet

Until
forbidden things
lean against us

Our fingers
gently calling
to our hair

Our tongues
almost extinct

In the purity
that carries chance
a few moments forward

In the embrace
of each kiss
continued
past the grave

We are
without study
the animal that excites us

We are
at once pulled
out of the harness
of our bones

Sitting

She is bringing
her hand down

She has stopped waiting
for gravity

She is
no random number

She has caught
the motion
of a fish

She has opened
to the middle
of a word

She is changing
the distance

She is driving
with one hand

She is bringing
it down

She is doing it
She is doing it

Her eyes
are designs of heat

Her lips
are the breath
she is taking

She is bringing
it down

She is doing it

She is proud

She is too awake
to sleep

She is too alive
to die

She is bringing
it down to the cloth

She is shaking it out
through the soil

She is
up to the sky

She is bringing
it down

She is doing
it

No Dime

No dime
goes around
       dancing

give you up dead

No memorizer walks
down this sidewalk

give you up dead

Rain bust open

The wind pick up
its secret money

See you
   on the subway
ask you where
you live

Wish I could
loosen you

Write you all
these letters
to your house

When I was
sleeping it was morning

All these nights
stuck on you

All these
cutthroat chickens

A bum
on the sidewalk

Another bum
in a tree

A steelworker
I bet he makes
good money

The Empire State Building

Give you up for dead
Next time I don't see you

Logging

The animal
is close

I call you out

You have taken
my body with
small teeth

You have died
in my childbirth

the wind
through the blue windows

the breath
choking on the skeleton

I call you out
I eat you back

Grandmother,
Your face biting
over mine

The house burning
secretly

The animal
closer

I call you back

Your son trembling
like someone about
to wake

Father

The words
      become speech

The dry seed
grows into stone

I let your death
sting me
again

I mark
your passing
with my face

Trading

Father
I cannot
hold your soul
any longer
Your flesh
is the marriage food
of the earth

Wolf
fox
and dog
You are believed

Daughter
and brother
Mother of capture

From generations
this rain
is born

go into
its shade

You are believed

Untitled

dressed the child
threw it in the air

saw a
very old face

outstretched
the knife

threw it in
the air

caught the
child

       over
the grave

caught the
knife

threw it
in the air

in the air
a ghost

in my heart
in the air
a ghost

kept it
in the
air

Muse #2

You belong
to the darkness
that is crossing to
your body

You belong
to the invisible system
of day

All the hills
have power

You belong
to a country
of someone else

These round stones
I lift up to you

Do not throw me
back under
the ground

Half And Half Again

Before the night

Before its confusion
of iron and silk

Before even one necklace
of sweat is wiped away

There is blood

Blood that the sea
has finished with

Blood that has
blown through the heart
and not come back

Before you speak

Before you imitate
the dead

Know
that the dead imitate nothing
And that blood
imitates only the sea

Before you mask
your teeth

Before you walk
back from sleep

Before even the moon
silvers over and you
see your face

Know that there are
two kinds of dead
And know that you
are one of them

Your Thick Hair
–for Garcia Lorca

Your thick hair
is a suitable hill

The soldiers that
came to take you
were curious and
afraid of its heat
and transmissions

The daylight you carried
had continued for years
it was clearly the work
of a dancer, an unknown
lover who had never forgotten
the two step

The news is clear
on this point

The poor are an
acceptable underwear
for the rich

Likewise the Moon
and the poets it claims
to represent have let
themselves get walked over

They are swimming in
a sea of tranquillity

And we are out
everyday walking
against a new gravity

And we have in buildings
rocks from the moons'
openness

And we have in heavy bars
the gold from the teeth
of all those Jews

and in jails
sit the men and women
who have satisfied our justice

Lorca
We are looking
for the road

The road that goes
through the forest
of our poems

The road that goes
through the house of
the liar who really wants
nothing except to lie

The road over
the fallen angels
through the fields
of the butchers

The butchers who
will cut the fat
from our tongues
for a price

Lorca
The road that comes out
next to the eye
of the Fascist

Next to
the fear of
the poem

Next to
the fear of
the poetry inside
the people

Next to
the fear that together
we are sharpening
the truth into a blade

Lorca
Your thick hair is
a suitable hill from
which to see this
countryside

Crescent

The clouds
take up
the surface
of the light

Among the trees
there is suddenly
a clearing

And then your blood
is speaking to
your mouth

And then your mouth
is your companion

You give
your life
to this

You throw
away
your luck

The night
is all along
your skin

The path ahead
is lit
with darkness

Anywhere

dog
loves a
dog
or
its bite
or the sequence
of its heat
or the
sound it makes
as it
eludes another dog

sex
to have it
even hidden bones
breaking

dog
all its life
out
of its skin
coming
to bark
another
into barking
dog

Dance #2

With their hands
they come dancing

With their singing
their furious singing

They leap
they swing open
a wind in
every direction
A birth

Some of them
a taste

Some of them
the full mouth
of a god

They are like
the water you
are just now swallowing
They are like
the bite of
the loved animal

look at them

they surrender nothing

they are each other
as they remember

Down

Two oxen of blood
pull my mouth
from yours

Two simple songs
go down my tongue
as I go down on yours

As I go down
on you
the dark sings
the dark pulls up
its roots

Your sex
all color and
shimmering

Your sex
as warm
as your mouth

You are naming
visions in this darkness

You are voicing
          pleasure
to give it voice

Your sex
down to
a thick mist

Your sex carrying you
almost as far as
it goes

Someone seeks
a boat
and water

Someone terrifies
the dead

Two people
leave each others' sleep
and go on waking

Two people
finish off the night
without their skin

Blessing

Now sleep

Little bits of wax
over your eyes

The worst fish
raging in your mouth

Now wake
in reverse

Now hold
the place
of your body

recall
the strangers face

suffer this
and the flight
of birds above you

Now the real moon
is seen
And now
the Sun

Now the flight
of leaves

The trees
storm the brain

And then
you are the source
of all water

And then
you are the stone
that fills the ground
with light

Place

I am as
ready as death

On this side
that the blood takes

On this side
that keeps turning
from the eye

Where the light
has fallen

Where the dark
has climbed between
the living and the dead

I am as far
as the blind spot

As far as the words
that lay closed
on my tongue

As the wind
rushes to enter the stone

As the moon
impersonates the sun

So much wants to
show itself

So much returns
to reoccur

I am with the children
in the open truck
as we stop for gas

I am with the old ones
as we cross the
current of the road
to the harvest

Poem For A Cuban Brigade
Of Women Cane Cutters

Single
divorced
married
child bearing
child heavy
child light
Stevedores of Revolution
muscled
in the sun, in the motion
of morning machetes
cutting into cane

Cane Cutters
27 in this Brigade
the youngest 15
the oldest 54
with the courage
of anything
Afterall
women can do
anything
Cutting early light
and dusk
emptying the work
from the land
Heroes of the Harvest

The women
in the fields

The rivers
of their effort

Each of them
one body
of water

All of them
together
the sea

Pursuit

No one
fire escapes you
no unimagined cloud
sentimental lover
step of a
dance
             of a family
no one sits through this
no one
feels the road ending
suddenly the car
your dreams
no one catches them
catches up
you ride
one hand
rolling down the window
your neck
shaking off its light

Lines

Here is the morning
attached to
the night

The trees
dropping branches
to the wind

Here is time
licking its tongue
across a knife

Your body
the stretch of it
as tempered
as the light

Here are
my palms
your thighs
the noise
as the earth
lays us down
to its need

Here is what
holds us

The miles
of root

The cold
and the heat

The sun
left behind
by the moon

Inside

Inside me

A blind dog
A mountain soaked
in stone

Inside you

A delicate bullet
A huge wing folding
and unfolding

Sudden
Suddenly
the blood is released
or advanced between us

Somewhere
like us
an old plow comes back
to the surface

Somewhere
like us
An animal dies
and feels it and feels itself
become cold meat

We obey the city
We continue to transmit
its alphabet

Inside me

A fragment of wind
A language resting
on the dead

Inside you

The skeleton of
a sun
A razor armed with
its own life

City Night

One bone
now comes to rest
against another

This is one meal

The moon is played out

The clouds go back
inside the dead

This is one room

Now the street backs away
from the houses

Now the wind feels its way
to the corners

Under the haze
of electricity

Under all the individual
spots of blood

The cars
are jumping for it

The windows are
gathering glass

The night
breaks wide open

The stars
they lower down
until they are even
with our faces
then they slash
with their light

Open

We look,
words break
off
bits of light
the ground
is
a kind of sky
of little things
our lives
rush up to meet us
loving to
hold us
our bodies
kiss us
halfway

Friday

These children
walk by
with their souls
made of water

they are
conceived of,
moving
deliveries of light
and color

they
roll down
the hills

these children
combine us
in their solitude

see how
everything
splashes
around them

their hands
first holding

their voices
working over
and over

they name
each thing
they love

Stop

The air hits
our Mother tongue
We talk
in its stride
about death
and astonishment

We sit
and the words
take us under
and the silence
spills back
to our ears

liked even
what name you
went under
when you went
I like even
the way I'll
never find you

The child
comes up
comes up
just to hug

The sidewalk
has the earth
below it
the sun
puts the fix on
      you move
above it

Taking Out The Bronx

This is one brilliant morning
of Detroit

This is the day shift

And all the holders of sweat
are up and blessing
their throats with coffee

And all the radio dials
are giving off enough light
to dress by

This is the 5:30 AM street
laid down around every
house

This is Detroit
parked like a car
next to a lake

This is Detroit
on its back
in the morning

Detroit
like all the different
parts of a gun laid out,
separated on a map
and oiled

Detroit
the goddess of
its own eyes

And all the muscles
tighten towards
the heart here

All the dead are
fitted with extra teeth

Detroit
the way it coaxes
more dark each morning
The way the clouds
always float face down

This is the city of Detroit
and within it a strange
game of mounting traffic

This is Detroit and Detroit
is the curve in the road
that takes you like a
breast into the mouth of work

Calling

We are calling
each other
by name
by the definite numbers
of the clock

one morning
and then a clearing
of silence
two hours
two less

A pure fish
on your spine
A letter of alphabets
traveling to your hand

You divide
with me

The suck
of words

The hard memory,
meaning blood

The root
stranded in the air

You divide
what happens
the night
happens

You divide
what divides us
from sleep

Meeting

The Sun is dark

The wind behind it,
is radiant

The woman is singing

She sings over the earth
and the earth pushes up
its dreams

The woman sleeps openly

It is dark
where she sleeps
but the Sun is there

Something is shaking

dead star
alive or breathing

break in the neck

rattle of words

Someone is,
The man is singing

He is singing and
the drum of his skin
is beating, the dream
is sweating out from his
insides

He is waking
and the dead expect to see him

a voice,
then nothing

It is light
when he wakes
but the moon is there

He goes out

Shows his face
to the fire

And they walk

Untitled

You jump over the fire

Black waist
of the water

Dogs run next to me

I run alongside you
I kiss your face

I would tell you
everything now

I would bend down
and become the blood
that leaves you

laughing, you say
my name

You bite with
your absolute teeth

Your hair flies
upward over my face

This is just where
you would take me

I bend down

Here

The animal offers
itself

The land
obeys itself

Where we lay
has covered our bodies

What we own
could be owned
by horses

This place is
so much
like another

it makes us
want to talk

Turning

There are
certain dreams
on certain nights,
that never happen

There are
combinations of numbers
that refuse to break up
and combinations
of words that become
deadfalls

There are certain dreams
on certain nights

There are things
you can't remember
because you have
become the memory

There are animals
you can't bring down
because you would
fall with them

There are dangers
you can't calculate

There are places
towards which
your arms reach
that would
hold you forever

Places on either side
that you have to
come back from

And there are the living
and the dead

And these too are combinations

Alone

You walk
along the coast,
some shoreline
that you want to bridge

So that
the wind
won't leave
your side

So that
the clouds
will travel with you
like a pack of dogs

Your own voice
keeps you
until you
let it fall

All the threads
in your words
breaking

All the parts
of the water
coming to touch
your mouth

And the one
who comes
to rescue you
loses sight

And the best
that is done
is just to join you

Back there
your only enemy
was someone worse
than you were

Back there
you never
woke up
this side
of you

Of The Mother

The anger

The tree
is buried

its roots
are branches,
its branches
are one quick
slap from our faces

The light
this same light
reaches

the ones who
are fish take honey
from the tree

the ones who grind
the water lose their
throats to the tree

In the light
The same light

On the heads
of the newborn children,
the same light

In order to
lose this we
must wash
with salt

What will
we eat

The fruit of the
tree is in the mouth
of the Mother

Calendar

I bring your hands
to my face

I spit you out
Murder

I spit you out
A Jar Of Flame

I spit you out
a tongue that was
never sewn together

I kneel

I blow on
the heat

I use my pulse
like a candle
like a prayer that
repeats itself

I stay here

I know the living
I know the dying
I know the dead

by their hunger
by their fingers
by the way they
sit up and eat

I know this day

I know this place
I know you

The Dead

We roll together

We become the color
of haystack and stone

And the next eye
of the blind

And the next
voice of the dumb

Asleep
we prepare
to console the living

Asleep
we recognize our bodies
and play dead

And we are
blown away from
each other

We spread into fire

We burn up
in the dark
in the night
in the kitchen
along with all that
is restless, all that
moves in the heat and
dreams

We are not waiting
for the light

The light
turns below us

We live
over
the edge of something
and we sleep someplace
but not lying down

Poem

This paper
the words
pulled to it
A field
the Sun
in it
the overflow
of light
The rocks,
the trees
marked with chalk
the animal
somewhere
Want to lay down
to it
Want to cut
through it
This spot
in the open
the dead
somewhere
the smell of them
coming downwind

Rape

bite of cunt
to this man
who wants
to break your body
to his cock

who wants
to kill you
every month
period

And it becomes
a highway of cars
The lights go by

A highway
down to a spoon

Remembering
the ground
underground

shooting ground

The woman
beaten in the belly
around the head
inside

The woman
held down
on
his body

Taste of vomit

Passage #2

The diamond cuts
the nerve in two

The trees struggle
with the wind

Something pulls,
something comes
to be death

And the body is out of reach
The body is still at sea

It is good

You die now
You swallow the root

And the body loves it

The body gives all
movement to it

And the light sucks
through the body

And the body fills up
and goes away

except
the light
the light stays in the bone,
it is tremendous

Wanted

We are alone
on the steps

We are robbed
on the road

We are senseless
on the bridge

We are alive
in the struggle

We occupy the pavement

We pick up
the child

The work

The hardest
work

The work
that doesn't care
for any voice

The work
that stops
us

Honor it
with me

Terms

The Sun is your boat

The Moon, it is only dreaming

Your Name
Your Name

A knife could pass between us
Only the water is as beautiful

Your Name
Your Name

You choose what delights you

You choose what is fire
even if it seems cold

And your arms are all blue,
made of feathers

And your face is not tied
to any bone

Your Name
Your Name

There is no hiding place

There is no star
that rises without light

Your Name
Your Name

I lift my tongue
to turn it over

I open my flesh
to catch your seed

Untitled

the sun moves
more quietly
than we can even hear

the sun
moves along its path
of firewood

You wake

I turn to see
the light on your body

I turn to listen
to your breath
spinning out of sleep

Your arms open
my arms

There are no words
to this

It is quieter
than we can even hear

Terms #3

I am anxious
and wild

It is your drifting
body

It is your
constant birth

All the pain
All the words

It is your hand
It is your moon

You the right eye
You the dog song

Without the sky
With only
the dark light

know me

I am here
for you

Jump against
my life

Beau Beausoleil was born in 1941 in the Bronx, New York.
He has lived in San Francisco since 1969.